D0244443
BIRR
26 AUG 2020
WITHDRAWN

PROJECT GEOGRAPHY

The Sea

Written by Sally Hewitt

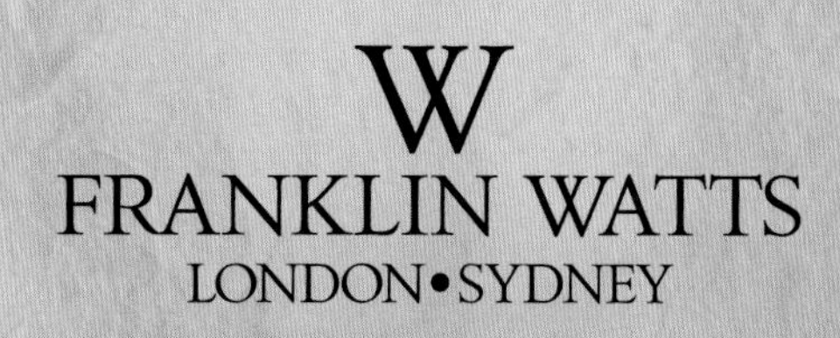
W
FRANKLIN WATTS
LONDON•SYDNEY

First published as *Starting Geography: By the Sea* in 2009 by Franklin Watts. This edition 2012

338 Euston Road, London NW1 3BH

Franklin Watts Australia
Hachette Children's Books
Level 17/207 Kent Street, Sydney NSW 2000

Copyright © Franklin Watts 2009

Editor: Katie Dicker
Art Direction: Dibakar Acharjee (Q2AMedia)
Designer: Tarang Saggar (Q2AMedia), Shweta Nigam (Q2AMedia)
Picture researcher: Kamal Kumar (Q2AMedia)
Craft models made by: Jyotsna Julka (Q2AMedia), Shweta Nigam (Q2AMedia)
Photography: Tarang Saggar (Q2AMedia)

Picture credits:
t=top b=bottom c=centre l=left r=right

Cover: PhotoAlto/Sigrid Olsson/Jupiter Images
Title page: Audrey M Vasey/Shutterstock, Tischenko Irina/Shutterstock.
Insides: Hubert Stadler/Corbis: 6, John Hemmings/123rf: 7t, Graeme Knox/Shutterstock: 7b, Petros Tsonis/Shutterstock: 9tr, Albert Barr/Shutterstock: 10, KeithBinns/Istockphoto: 11tr, Carlos Caetano/Shutterstock: 12l, M.A.C./Shutterstock: 12r, Karin Lau/Shutterstock: 13tr, CruxPhotos/Istockphoto: 14, Joe Gough/Shutterstock: 15tr, Dchadwick/Istockphoto: 16, Liseykina/Shutterstock: 17tr, Angelo Cavalli/Robert Harding World Imagery/Corbis: 18, Sasha/Fotolia: 19tr, Tom Ang/Fotolia: 20, Cyrille Lips/123rf: 21tr, Joel W. Rogers/Corbis: 22, DJMattaar/Istockphoto: 23tr, PhotoAlto/Sigrid Olsson/Jupiter Images: 24, Audrey M Vasey/Shutterstock: 25t, Deborah Wolfe/Shutterstock: 25bl, Adisa/Shutterstock: Kim Ruoff/Shutterstock: 25br, Danny Lehman/Corbis: 26, Nik Wheeler/Corbis: 27tr, Aditya Kok/123rf: 27bl, Matthew Gough/Shutterstock: 27br.
Q2AMedia Image Bank: Imprint page, Contents page, 9, 11, 13, 15, 17, 21, 23.
Q2AMedia Art Bank: 8, 19.

With thanks to our models Shruti Aggarwal, Jyotsna Julka

Every attempt has been made to clear copyright. Should there be any inadvertent omission please apply to the publisher for rectification.

A CIP catalogue record for this book is available from the British Library

ISBN: 978 1 4451 0937 4

Dewey Classification: 577.69'9

Printed in China
Franklin Watts is a division of Hachette Children's Books, an Hachette UK company.
www.hachette.co.uk

Leabharlann
Chontae Uíbh Fhailí
Class: J333.9
Acc: 12/10826
Inv: 12/364
8.73

Contents

The seashore

The place where the land meets the sea is called the coast or the seashore. A seashore might be steep cliffs, a rocky beach, a sandy shore or a muddy **estuary**.

A seaside town has hotels for people to stay in, cafés and restaurants, and beach huts or sun umbrellas for shade.

At the beach

Beaches are made of soft sand or large pebbles. They form when the wind and waves push sand and stones against the land. Beaches are often gently sloping. They are popular places on a hot day because swimmers can get in and out of the water easily.

Cliffs

Cliffs are where the land drops steeply down to the sea. Cliffs can be made of hard rocks or soft sand and mud. Over many years, cliffs are worn away by the wind, rain and waves.

The white cliffs of Dover on the south coast of England are made of chalk.

Estuaries

An estuary is where a river flows into the sea and mixes fresh water with salty sea water. The river drops mud on its way to the sea, making this coastal area quite flat.

Birds use their long, pointed beaks to search through the estuary mud for worms and shellfish.

Coasts

The sea covers two-thirds of planet Earth. It meets the land along 440,000 kilometres of coast. Canada is the country with the longest coast, stretching 243,791 kilometres.

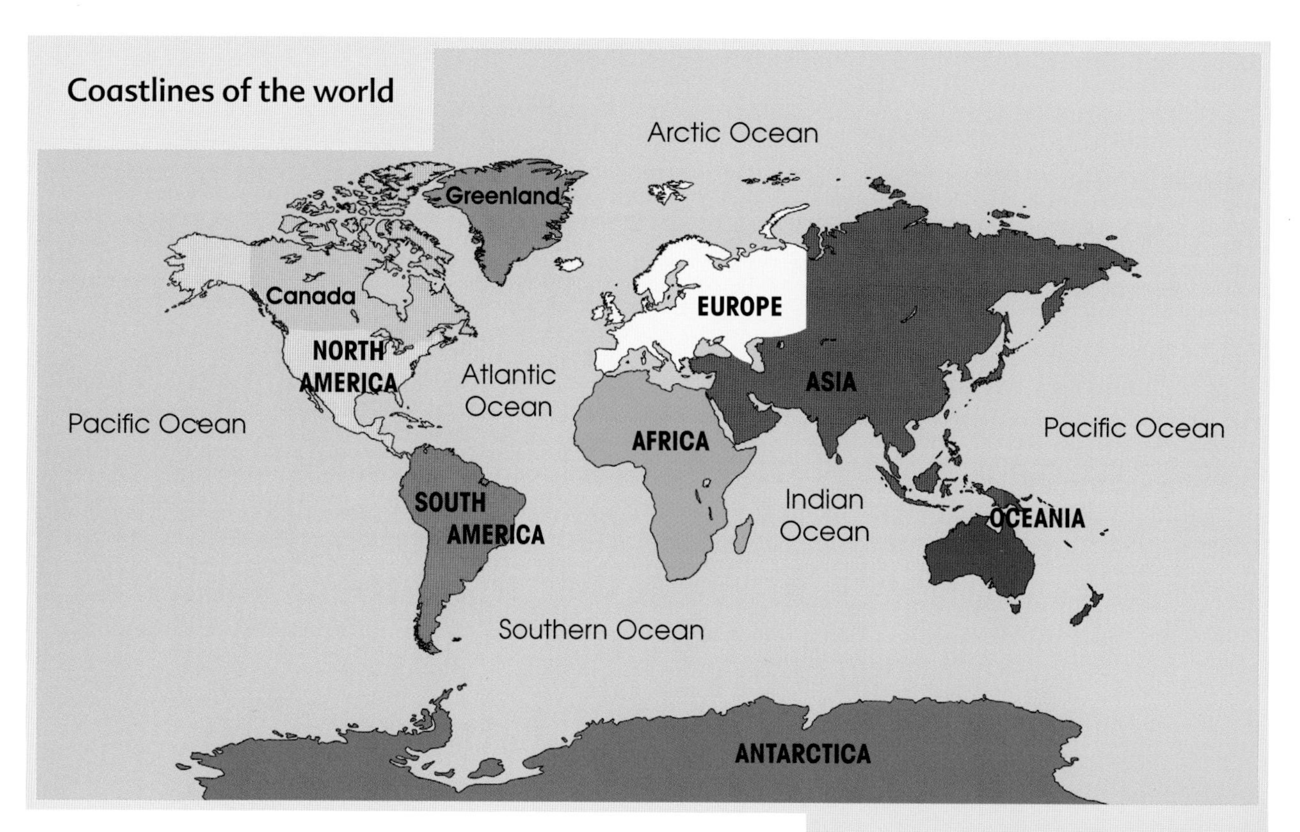

The Earth has five oceans that surround seven large pieces of land called 'continents'. There are also many smaller seas.

Changing coasts

Coasts are constantly changing shape because sea water moves, carving out **bays** and **inlets** and building up beaches. This means that the shape of islands and countries changes, too.

Islands

An island is an area of land surrounded by water. Wherever you are on an island, you are probably not far away from the coast. Greenland is the biggest island on Earth.

The island of Santorini, Greece, was formed when a volcano erupted under the sea.

Create an island

You will need:

- glue • card
- string • scissors
- paints and paintbrushes

1 Cut a piece of string 66 cm long and tie the ends together, using about 6 cm for the knot.

2 Arrange the string on some card in the shape of an island with a crooked coastline, 60 cm long.

3 Use some glue to stick the string down.

4 Decide what kind of coast you have created and add labels such as sandy beach, cliffs, rocks, harbour, bay and estuary.

5 Paint your island and the sea around it. Add buildings, trees and other interesting features.

If 1 cm = 1 km, how long is the coastline of your island?

Harbours

A bay, where the coast curves inwards, can form a natural harbour. Harbours are places where ships and boats can sail close to shore and put down their anchors in calm, sheltered waters.

A ferry carries passengers on short trips across water. Cars and trucks use a slope to drive on and off the ferry.

Ports

Many towns have grown up around ports. A port has **docks** where ships can load and unload their **cargo** and people can get on and off the boats. A harbour wall protects ships and boats from crashing waves.

Keeping ships safe

Lighthouses are sometimes found at the mouth of a harbour. The light at the top of a lighthouse flashes all day and all night. It tells sailors where the harbour mouth is. Other lighthouses warn sailors away from dangerous rocks.

This lighthouse warns passing ships to stay away from the rocks.

Make a model lighthouse

You will need:

- sheet of A4 white card
- scissors • sticky tape
- red paint • circle of foil
- clear plastic cup • torch

1 Cut the card as shown. Roll it to make a cone with an open top and tape the two sides together.

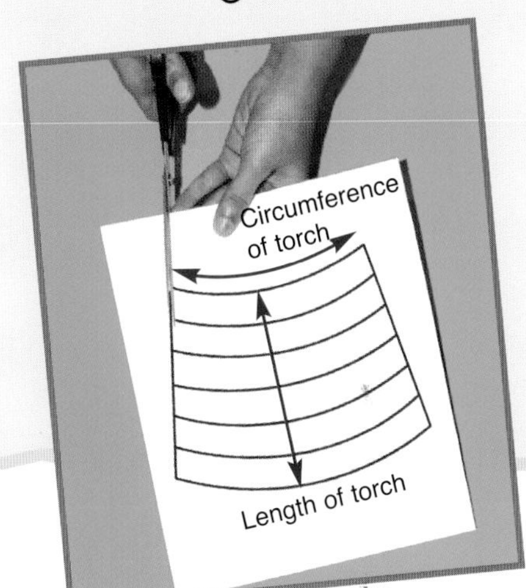

2 Paint red stripes around the cone.

3 Push the foil circle into the bottom of the cup to make a reflector.

4 Push the cup into the cone so the closed end sticks out at the top. Tape the cup in place if needed.

5 Turn on the torch (use the flashing setting if possible) and place the cone over it.

Tides

Tides are caused by the **gravity** of the Moon pulling on the ocean water. There are usually two high tides and two low tides every 24 hours.

Between the tides

As the tide goes in and out, part of the seashore is repeatedly covered and uncovered by water. The sea drops seaweed, shells and litter along the **high tide mark.**

At high tide, the sea moves high up the beach.

At low tide, the sea moves back, uncovering sand or rock pools.

Beach life

Lots of plants and animals live between the high tide mark and the edge of the sea at low tide. They have **adapted** to survive on land and under water.

A sea anemone clings to a rock so that it is not swept out to sea.

Make a rock pool

You will need:
- books or magazines with pictures of rock pool animals
- self-hardening clay • water
- waterproof paint • tray or large bowl • rocks and sand

1 Find pictures of rock pool animals such as starfish, sea anemones, shrimps, small fish and crabs.

2 Make clay models of these creatures and paint them.

3 To make a rock pool, line a tray or a large bowl with rocks and sand. Add some water.

4 Place your animals carefully in and around the pool. Bury a crab partly in sand and hide shrimps and starfish between rocks, for example.

5 Ask your friends to spot the rock pool animals.

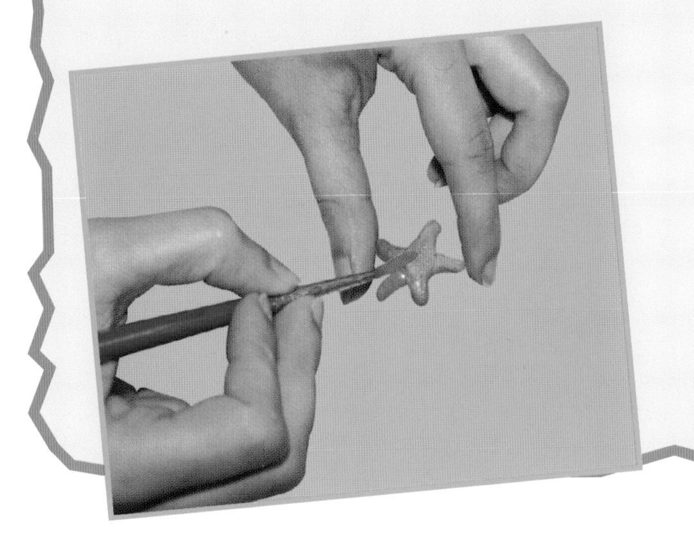

Wearing away

The shape of the coast is constantly changing. Waves drag sand and pebbles to and from the beach. The waves break off bits of rock as they crash against the cliffs.

A rough sea wears the coast away more quickly than a calm sea.

Waves

Sea water is never still. As the wind blows across its surface, it creates waves. Strong winds whip up huge waves, while light winds create gentle ripples. Waves created by storms can do a great deal of damage to the coast.

Collapsing cliffs

When waves break against the bottom of cliffs they wear the rocks away. Over time, the waves create an **overhang**. With nothing to support it, the top of the cliff collapses. Sometimes cliffs can be worn away to form arches or **stacks**.

Soft rock wears away faster than hard rock. This creates headlands, caves, arches and stacks.

Create a collapsing cliff

You will need:
- large tray • water
- sand, soil and stones

1 Build up a mixture of wet sand, soil and stones in the shape of a cliff, using about a quarter of the tray at one end.

2 Cover the bottom of the rest of the tray with about 2 cm of water.

3 Gently rock the tray so the water laps against the cliff.

4 See how the water wears away the cliff at the bottom, and the top falls into the water.

Building beaches

Sand is made up of tiny pieces of rock, shell and **coral** that have been broken up by the waves. A beach forms when the waves drop these tiny pieces onto the shore.

Sand dunes

The wind blows sand into mounds called dunes. A type of tough grass called marram that grows on dunes has deep, wide-spreading roots. It grows well by the sea and helps to hold the sand in place.

Without marram grass, the wind would blow the sand dunes away.

Pebbles

Beach pebbles are called shingle. The biggest pebbles are found at the top of the beach. They get smaller and smaller until they are just tiny specks at the water's edge. This is because the moving water wears the pebbles away.

Pebbles are small pieces of rock that have been smoothed and polished by the movement of waves.

Make some pebbles

You will need:
- self-hardening clay
- paints and paintbrush
- PVA glue • glass bowl or jar
- water

1 Roll lumps of self-hardening clay into smooth pebble shapes. Leave them to dry.

2 Use the picture above to give you ideas for colours and patterns and paint your pebbles.

3 When the paint is dry, varnish your pebbles with PVA glue mixed with water.

4 Put your pebbles in a glass bowl or jar and cover them in water to make a table decoration.

Human changes

When people live by the sea or visit the coast, they change the environment. Houses, hotels, car parks and cafés are built for people to use. Walkways are built on the beach and **piers** stick out into the sea.

Popular beaches have buildings and pathways for tourists to use.

Groynes and sea walls

Groynes and sea walls are features built at the coast. They stop natural changes made by the waves and the weather. Groynes are wooden fences built out into the sea to stop sand and pebbles being washed away. Sea walls protect seaside towns from storm waves.

Truckloads of sand

Sandy beaches are more popular than rocky or pebbly beaches. Sand is soft to walk on. It is good for sunbathing and useful for building sandcastles! Some beaches have sand added to them to attract visitors.

Extra sand is being added to this beach.

Find out how people change beaches

1 Look at the picture on page 18 or find a photograph of a popular beach.

2 Make a note of all the features that have been built.

3 Draw a picture of what you imagine the beach would look like without any buildings.

4 Which beach do you like best? Why?

Enjoying the sea

Swimming, snorkelling, sailing and surfing are just some of the water sports that take place near beaches. Sailing boats are kept in shallow water or stored in boathouses nearby.

Swimming safety

Buoys on the surface of the water show areas where it is safe to swim. Warning flags fly where rough seas and strong **currents** can pull swimmers, surfers and sailors under the water or out to sea.

Lifeguards keep watch for anyone in trouble or danger in the water.

Wind and waves

People who like water sports use the **energy** of the wind and the waves to power them across the water. Sails and kites catch the wind and surfboards ride the waves.

On windy days, the beach is a popular place for water sports.

Make a power kite

You will need:
- plastic carrier bag
- scissors • string • card
- sticky tape or glue

1 Cut through the middle of a plastic carrier bag to about 12 cm from the bottom.

2 Flatten out the bag with the handles at either end.

3 Flatten the 'bottom' of the bag and tape it down to strengthen the middle of your kite.

4 Stiffen your kite with three strips of card taped or glued across the width, one in the middle, the others 10 cm on either side.

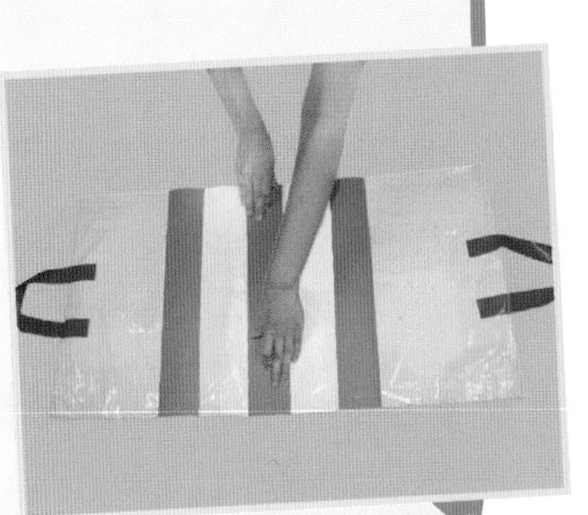

5 Tie 2 metres of string (or more) to each of the bag handles.

6 Fly your power kite on a windy day.

Fishing

The sea is full of fish and shellfish that are good for us to eat. Fishermen in small boats catch fish through the night. They bring their catch to shore to sell at early morning markets.

Factory ships

Some fishermen work on large factory ships. They prepare and freeze the fish they catch to keep it fresh. This means they can stay at sea for a long time.

In some oceans, we are catching too many fish and species are dying out.

Safety in numbers

Fish often swim together in big groups called shoals. Fishing boats drop their nets to find shoals of cod, herring and other fish we like to eat.

Fish swim in shoals to protect themselves from enemies.

Make a fish collage

You will need:

- scissors • sponge
- coloured tissue paper – green, blue, black, brown
- white paint • large sheet of blue paper • glue

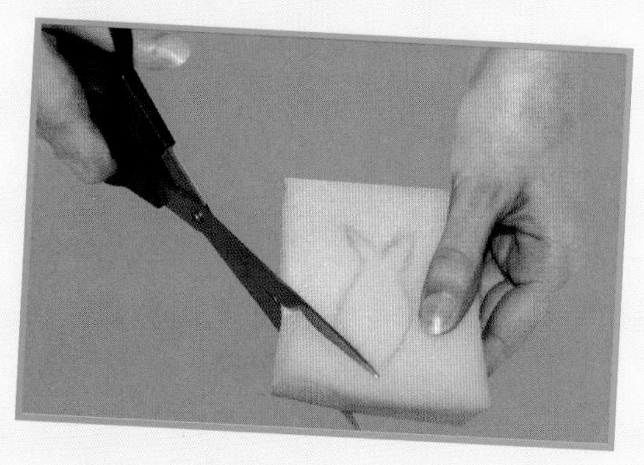

1 Cut the sponge into the shape of a fish.

2 Tear green and blue tissue paper into rough strips. Stick them onto the blue paper for an underwater effect.

3 Scrunch up the black tissue paper to make rocks and tear the brown tissue paper to make strands of seaweed. Stick them onto the bottom of the picture.

4 Dip the sponge into the white paint and print fish shapes on the tissue paper all facing the same direction, to look like a shoal of fish.

Seaside holidays

Seaside holidays are popular because there are so many things to do – from swimming in the sea and exploring rock pools, to building sandcastles, walking the cliff paths and taking part in water sports and ball games.

Keeping safe

In summer, the Sun can feel very hot. It can burn your skin. You should wear sun cream to protect your skin and cover yourself with a hat and light, loose clothing. Sunglasses also help to protect your eyes from the Sun's glare.

This family has brought a lot of equipment to the beach. They are having fun and keeping safe.

Plan a trip to the seaside

1 Look at a map to see how far you have to go.

   a) Can you get to the seaside and back in a day?

   b) If not, where will you stay?

   c) How will you get there – car, bus, train, aeroplane?

   d) Use a map and timetables to plan your route.

2 Make a list of all the things you will need to take. For example:

- clothes (including a sun hat)
- towels
- sun cream
- swimming costume
- bucket and spade
- kite
- book
- picnic (or money to buy food)
- water to drink
- a cool bag/box

Caring for the seaside

When we visit the seaside we can cause damage, but there are lots of things we can do to protect our beaches. Taking our litter home is one example. Litter is dirty, looks bad and can harm wildlife.

Wildlife at risk

Some beaches are protected to help the plants and animals that live there. Tourists can disturb animals and endanger wildlife without meaning to. We should keep to paths when we go walking and stay away from protected beaches.

Baby turtles hatch on the sand and make their way to the sea. Tourists can disturb this area.

Coral care

Many people like to snorkel or dive among rocks and coral. It is a good way to spot the colourful fish that live there. However, breaking off coral and disturbing rocks destroys these natural **habitats**.

Don't buy shells and coral. Rare animals may have been killed, habitats damaged and laws broken to collect them.

Get to know the coast

1 Visit a local stretch of coast or choose a coast anywhere in the world. Use books or ask an adult to help you use the Internet to find out more about it.

2 Choose one animal, one bird and one plant you would find there. What could you do to help protect them?

3 Draw up a table like the one below to show your suggestions.

Animal/Bird/Plant	Behaviour	What can I do?
Grey seal (animal)	• eats fish and shellfish near the shore • gives birth to pups on shore	• watch quietly from a distance • don't disturb while adults are feeding their pups
Oyster catcher (bird)	• uses long beak to eat mussels and worms in sand • lays eggs in pebbles	• keep off pebbles during the nesting season
Marram grass (plant)	• grows on sand dunes	• don't trample or uproot the grass (this will damage the dunes)

Glossary

adapted
A plant or an animal that has adapted has changed so it can live in a particular place. Crabs, for example, have adapted to live above and below water.

bay
A bay is an area of sea sheltered by a stretch of coastline that curves inland.

buoy
A buoy is a floating marker anchored to the seabed. Buoys with lights or bells guide and warn ships of danger.

cargo
Cargo is a ship's load of goods that it carries from one place to another.

coral
Coral grows in warm sea water. Living coral grows on top of coral skeletons and creates a coral reef.

current
A current is a steady flow of water moving in one direction.

docks
Docks are sheltered areas of water where ships are moored and people and cargo are loaded and unloaded.

energy
Energy is the power that makes things work. Yachts, windsurfers and surfboards use the energy of the wind and waves to move.

estuary
An estuary is a part of the coast where a river runs into the sea and fresh water and sea water mix.

gravity
Gravity is a natural force that pulls things down towards the ground.

groynes
Groynes are wooden fences built out into the sea to stop the beach from being washed away.

habitat
A habitat is the natural surroundings that are home to an animal or plant. For example, the seashore is the habitat of a crab.

high tide mark
A high tide mark is the highest point that the sea comes up a beach at high tide.

inlet
An inlet is a narrow band of sea water stretching inland from the coast.

lighthouse
A lighthouse is a tower or building with a bright light to warn or guide ships at sea.

overhang
An overhang is the top part of a cliff that sticks out over a space where the cliff underneath has worn away.

pier
A pier is a platform on stilts jutting out into the sea where boats can dock and people fish, walk and sit.

stack
A steep column of rock in the sea near the coast. Stacks are formed when coastal cliffs are worn away by moving sea water.

tide
The tide is the rise and fall of sea water up and down the beach. It is caused by the gravity of the Moon pulling on the water.

Index